DR. CHRISTOPHER BRYANT

With My Whole Mind

A Pentecostal Integration of the Mind in Worship

WIPF & STOCK · Eugene, Oregon

MY WHOLE MIND
A Pentecostal Integration of the Mind in Worship

Wipf & Stock
An Imprint of Wipf and Stock Publishers
199 W. 8th Ave., Suite 3
Eugene, OR 97401

www.wipfandstock.com

PAPERBACK ISBN: 979-8-3852-5283-1
HARDCOVER ISBN: 979-8-3852-5284-8
EBOOK ISBN: 979-8-3852-5285-5

Unless otherwise noted, all Scripture quotations are taken from the Authorized (King James) Version, which is in the public domain.

Quotations labeled NRSV are from the New Revised Standard Version Bible, copyright © 1989 National Council of the Churches of Christ in the United States of America. Used by permission. All rights reserved.

Typesetting by The C/Suite Group

To my wife, Dr. Maisha Bryant, whose steadfast devotion have sustained every phase of this journey; and to my children, Gracie and Haddie, whose bright curiosity and joyful laughter continually renew my purpose. To the SPS, without whom this book would not exist! And to David Ketter, for his discerning feedback and constant camaraderie; to Bishop David Maldonado, for his pastoral encouragement and spiritual mentorship; and to Dr. Tony Blair, for his visionary guidance and generous counsel.

Contents

1

The Question That Defined Faith

First-century Jerusalem was tense with religious division and political instability. The Jewish people lived under the weight of Roman occupation, their national identity bound inextricably to their covenantal faith. The Temple, towering at the city's heart, served as both a sacred site and a subtle protest—a place believed to house God's presence, even as Roman soldiers patrolled its courts. The religious landscape was deeply fragmented: the Pharisees, fiercely committed to preserving Jewish distinctiveness, promoted a strict observance of the Torah; the Sadducees, who held priestly power, rejected the resurrection and secured their position by cooperating with Roman rule; the Zealots envisioned violent revolt in hopes of national liberation; and the Essenes, disillusioned by institutional corruption, retreated into the wilderness to await divine intervention.

In this fractured climate, Jesus's rising influence provoked deep anxiety among religious elites. His reinterpretation of the Law, his miraculous acts, and his fellowship with tax collectors and sinners marked him as both a theological provocation and a political irritant. The episode in Mark 12 unfolds against this backdrop. Jesus had already overturned tables in the Temple—a symbolic indictment of the religious system. Now, his opponents sought to entrap him with crafted questions. The Sadducees had just posed a challenge concerning resurrection and marriage—less a sincere inquiry than an attempt to publicly discredit him. Yet Jesus silenced them, appealing to the Torah itself with precision and spiritual authority.

It is in the aftermath of this exchange that a scribe steps forward—not to ensnare, but seemingly to inquire. His question breaks the pattern of calculated hostility. "Which commandment is the most important of all?" (Mark 12:28).

This was not a casual query. The Torah contained 613 commandments—248 positive, 365 prohibitive—and Jewish tradition wrestled with their proper ordering and relative weight. To ask which was greatest was to probe the very heart of Israel's covenant identity. As Kim Huat Tan notes, the scribe's question was a search for "the essence of orthodoxy and orthopraxy"—right belief wedded to right action.[1]

Jesus's response would not merely clarify the heart of Jewish devotion. It would articulate a theological center that would come to shape the worship of the early Church and the formation of Christian life. For Pentecostals, this exchange is especially resonant. It confronts the false binary between emotional fervor and intellectual engagement. Jesus's answer offers a vision of worship that joins spiritual passion with thoughtful reflection, inner fire with theological clarity.

The Response

Jesus's response would have been immediately recognizable to any Jewish listener. He quotes the Shema,[2] the central confession of Jewish faith: "Hear, O Israel: The Lord our God, the Lord is one. You shall love the Lord your God with all your heart, and with all your soul, and with all your mind, and with all your strength" (Mark 12:29–30 NRSV). The Shema was recited daily by devout Jews and represented the foundation of Jewish identity and devotion. But Jesus does something striking—he adds a word not found in the Masoretic

---

[1] Tan, "The Shema and Early Christianity," 186.

[2] The same conversation is had in Matthew 22:37. Jesus also has a similar conversation with a lawyer in Luke 10:25-28.

Text or the Targums and only tentatively present in the Septuagint:[3] mind. This subtle but profound addition reshapes the understanding of devotion, emphasizing the importance of intellectual engagement as a distinct and essential part of loving God.

The command to love God with one's heart in Jewish thought refers to the center of both emotion and thought. In the Hebrew mind, the heart was not merely the seat of feelings—it was the locus of intention, decision, and understanding. To love God with the heart, then, meant to direct one's innermost self toward God with sincerity and devotion. The term soul extended this idea to include the whole of one's being, encompassing the spiritual and existential dimensions of life. To love God with one's strength pointed to the physical and practical aspects of devotion—serving God through action and commitment in daily life.

But why add mind? If the heart already encompassed thought and understanding,[4] why introduce the mind as a separate category? The addition of mind functions to distinguish the intellectual faculties from the emotional and volitional ones. Jesus's inclusion of the mind elevates intellectual engagement as an essential part of devotion. It suggests that theological reflection, critical thinking, and the pursuit of knowledge are not peripheral to faith—they are integral to it. Loving God with the mind requires a commitment to study, to understanding, and to exploring the depths of God's revelation through Scripture and creation.

This is especially meaningful for Pentecostals, who have often been accused of emotionalism or anti-intellectualism. Jesus's expansion of the Shema challenges the idea that faith is purely experiential or mystical. It insists that loving God must involve the full range of human faculties: emotional, spiritual, intellectual, and practical. Worship is not diminished when it is thoughtful, nor is theological reflection weakened by emotional passion. True devotion requires both the heart and the mind in concert.

---

[3] "other interpretations of the period (LXX "force;" Qumran/rabbinic "wealth" or "property")," quoted in Lad, "Why Add 'and with All Your Mind'?"

[4] Stein, *Mark.*

Pentecostal Worship and the Life of the Mind

In Pentecostal and Charismatic traditions, the affective dimension of worship is often most visible. Charismatic worship is marked by emotional expression—raised hands, tears, shouting, speaking in tongues, and spontaneous prophecy. Pentecostal services often feature dramatic preaching styles and a fluid, unscripted liturgy that responds to the movement of the Spirit. The Pentecostal encounter with God is often visceral, embodied, and deeply emotional.

Critics have sometimes labeled this emotional intensity as "emotionalism" or even theological shallowness. But to reduce Pentecostal worship to mere emotionalism overlooks the theological depth that often underlies these expressions. The power of Pentecostal worship stems from an unmediated sense of divine presence—an immediacy with the Holy Spirit that transcends intellectual articulation. Yet the inclusion of the mind in the Great Commandment calls Pentecostals to go further.

Loving God with the mind means that theological reflection should not be a postscript to worship but an essential part of it. The same Spirit who inspires prophecy and tongues also inspires theological insight and understanding. Paul's admonition to pray with both the spirit and the understanding (1 Corinthians 14:15) reflects this balance. Pentecostal worship can—and should—be both ecstatic and thoughtful. A Spirit-filled life should reflect not only emotional intimacy with God but also intellectual engagement with his truth.

Bridging the Gap Between Head and Heart

The Great Commandment thus serves as a foundational text for bridging the gap between charismatic experience and intellectual rigor. It rejects the false dichotomy between head and heart, between study and prayer, and between the academy and the altar. Jesus's expansion of the Shema signals that devotion without understanding is incomplete—and understanding without devotion is lifeless. Theological depth does not threaten spiritual authenticity;

it enhances it.

For Pentecostals, this means that the pursuit of knowledge is not a threat to faith but a fulfillment of it. Engaging the mind in theological study, ethical reflection, and scriptural exegesis is itself an act of worship. Likewise, charismatic experience should not be regarded as intellectually inferior—it is a different but equally vital mode of knowing and loving God. The Great Commandment calls believers to embody a faith that is both passionate and thoughtful, a worship that is both emotional and reflective.

This integrated approach challenges contemporary Pentecostals to recover the life of the mind as a vital component of spiritual formation. Churches that foster both emotional engagement and theological depth will find themselves better equipped to disciple believers in a complex and intellectually demanding world. A balanced Pentecostal faith is one that prays in tongues and studies Scripture, that prophesies and reflects, that dances and discerns.

Reflection Questions

1. How does the inclusion of the mind in the Great Commandment challenge your current understanding of worship and devotion?
2. In what ways can Pentecostal churches cultivate both theological reflection and charismatic experience in their worship practices?
3. What steps can you take to deepen your intellectual engagement with God without losing the emotional intimacy of worship?
4. How can you integrate the head and the heart in your daily walk with God?
5. How might loving God with all your mind shape your approach to Scripture, prayer, and theological study?

2

With the Spirit and the Understanding

Ancient Corinth was a thriving urban center situated between two seaports, making it one of the most cosmopolitan and economically vibrant cities in the Roman Empire. Known for its wealth, diversity, and moral laxity, Corinth attracted traders, philosophers, and religious pilgrims from all over the Mediterranean world. It was a city of temples and theaters, markets and mysteries—a melting pot of cultures and ideologies. In this bustling environment, the church in Corinth was born, planted by the apostle Paul during his second missionary journey.

The Corinthian believers were charismatic, enthusiastic, and spiritually gifted. Paul commends them for not lacking in any spiritual gift (1 Corinthians 1:7), and their gatherings were marked by an intense expectation of God's presence. Yet alongside this spiritual vitality was a concerning lack of order. Their public worship had become a unintelligible noise—tongues spoken without interpretation, prophetic words delivered over one another, and practices that often obscured the communal purpose of worship. The gifts of the Spirit were present, but the fruits of the Spirit—like patience, gentleness, and self-control—were sometimes lacking in the public expression of those gifts.

Paul's first letter to the Corinthians is both pastoral and theological. He addresses their divisions, immorality, and theological confusion, but he dedicates significant attention to their worship practices. Chapter 14, in particular, becomes a crucial text for understanding how spiritual gifts should function within the gathered community. Paul is not interested in suppressing charismatic expression—far from it. He writes, "I thank God that I speak in tongues more than all of you" (1 Corinthians 14:18), and he expresses his desire that "all of you speak in tongues" (v. 5). Despite this, he is deeply concerned with the intelligibility and edifying nature of worship. His aim is to restore the balance between ecstatic experience and rational clarity, between individual spirituality and corporate benefit.

It is in this context that Paul offers a guiding principle that resonates deeply with Pentecostal worship today: "I will pray with the spirit, but I will pray with the understanding also; I will sing with the spirit, but I will sing with the understanding also" (1 Corinthians 14:15). With this declaration, Paul affirms a model of worship that is both spiritually vibrant and intellectually engaged—a vision that challenges Pentecostal communities to bring their hearts and minds fully into the presence of God.

The Balance Between Ecstasy and Intelligibility

Paul's theological insight into worship finds its clearest expression in 1 Corinthians 14:15: "I will pray with the spirit, but I will pray with the understanding also; I will sing with the spirit, but I will sing with the understanding also." Here, Paul articulates a dual approach to worship that engages both the spiritual and intellectual faculties. Prayer and praise are not merely emotional or ecstatic experiences—they are also intellectual acts that require understanding and reflection.

Importantly, Paul's argument is not only about the experience of the speaker but also about the experience of the hearer. Speaking in tongues, while spiritually edifying for the individual, leaves the congregation unedified unless the speech is interpreted. The issue is not whether tongues are rational or irrational; it is whether they are intelligible to the gathered community. When the mind is not engaged—whether in the speaker or the hearer—the result is spiritual isolation rather than communal edification.

Paul's distinction is subtle but profound. A person who speaks in tongues may experience personal spiritual uplift, but if their words are unintelligible to others (and even to themselves), the mind remains unfruitful (v. 14). The problem is not the absence of rational engagement in the act of speaking; the problem lies in the reception of the message. Paul's solution is not to forbid tongues but to insist that they be interpreted. In this way, both the speaker and the hearer are engaged intellectually and spiritually.

This insight has direct implications for Pentecostal worship. Pentecostal and charismatic traditions often prioritize the ecstatic dimension of worship—praying in tongues, prophetic utterances, and spontaneous expressions of praise. But Paul's teaching insists that true worship requires both spirit and understanding. The goal is not to diminish the emotional intensity of worship but to ensure that it is comprehensible and spiritually edifying for the gathered community.

Worship as Both Personal and Communal

One of the striking aspects of Paul's teaching on worship is the dual purpose it serves. Worship is first and foremost directed toward God. It is an offering of praise and devotion to the One who is worthy. God is both the object and the subject of our worship—our adoration is directed toward Him, and He is actively present in the midst of the worshiping community.

But worship also serves a communal function. Through worship, the people of God are instructed, encouraged, and shaped in their understanding of God's nature and will. Paul underscores this homiletical aspect of worship when he writes, "The one who prophesies speaks to people for their strengthening, encouraging and comfort" (v. 3). In other words, worship is not merely about personal encounter with God; it is also about the building up of the body of Christ.

For this communal dimension of worship to be effective, intelligibility is essential. Speaking in tongues may bless the individual, but it does not teach the gathered community unless the meaning is made clear. Paul's emphasis on prophecy stems from this principle: prophecy communicates a clear message that engages both the mind and the heart, resulting in communal edification.

The purpose of worship is not only to encounter God but to understand and respond to Him.

Paul's framework for worship, therefore, reflects the holistic nature of human devotion. Just as the Great Commandment calls believers to love God with heart, soul, mind, and strength, Pauline worship calls for engagement of the spirit and the understanding. True worship is not a choice between emotional experience and intellectual reflection—it is the integration of both dimensions.

The Intellectual Dimension of Pentecostal Worship

Paul's emphasis on intelligibility challenges Pentecostals to reconsider the role of the mind in worship. Pentecostal spirituality has long been characterized by its openness to the movement of the Spirit—prayer in tongues, prophecy, healing, and spontaneous expressions of praise. These practices reflect a deep commitment to the immediacy of God's presence and power. But Paul's teaching reminds Pentecostals that the intellectual dimension of worship is not secondary—it is essential.

Engaging the mind in worship does not mean suppressing charismatic experience. It means creating a space where the Spirit's movement is comprehensible and meaningful to the whole community. This can take the form of interpretation of tongues, structured teaching, reflective preaching, and the thoughtful ordering of worship. Worship that engages both spirit and mind creates a context where the presence of God is experienced emotionally and understood intellectually.

This integration is vital for the health of the Pentecostal church. A purely ecstatic worship experience may leave the mind disengaged and the congregation uninstructed. On the other hand, a purely intellectual approach to worship risks losing the transformative power of spiritual encounter. Paul's vision of worship invites Pentecostals to embrace both dimensions—to worship God with the mind fully engaged and the spirit fully alive.

Spirit and Understanding: A Model for Worship

Paul's solution to the Corinthian dilemma—worshiping with both spirit and understanding—offers a model for the modern church. In many contemporary contexts, worship has become polarized: either it is dominated by emotional expression with little intellectual content, or it is structured and intellectual but emotionally lifeless. Paul's model challenges these false dichotomies and calls the church to pursue a balanced, integrated form of worship.

When believers pray and sing with both spirit and understanding, worship becomes a complete act of devotion. The Spirit engages the heart and spirit, while understanding engages the mind. The mind reflects on the truth of God's word, while the spirit responds in faith and adoration. This dynamic relationship between spirit and understanding creates a worship experience that is both emotionally authentic and intellectually rich.

This balanced approach also reflects the broader theological vision of Paul's teaching. For Paul, worship is not merely a human act—it is a participation in the divine life. Through the Spirit, believers are drawn into the life of the Trinity, encountering God in ways that transcend rational comprehension while remaining rooted in theological truth. Worship that engages both spirit and understanding reflects the nature of this encounter, embodying the fullness of human devotion and divine revelation.

Reflection Questions

1. How does Paul's emphasis on both spirit and understanding reshape your view of Pentecostal worship?
2. In what ways can Pentecostal churches promote both charismatic experience and theological reflection in their worship practices?
3. How can you cultivate a worship life that engages both your spirit and your mind?
4. How does intelligibility in worship affect the spiritual growth of the congregation?

5. What steps can you take to ensure that your worship is both spiritually vibrant and intellectually engaging?

3

Learning as the Pursuit of God

The Roman Empire of the fourth century stood at a crossroads. Politically fragile, culturally diverse, and religiously pluralistic, the empire was in the midst of seismic transitions. Christianity had moved from the margins to the center of Roman life, following Constantine's conversion and the Edict of Milan in 313 AD. Yet pagan philosophy, imperial politics, and theological conflict still shaped the intellectual atmosphere. Into this complex world was born Aurelius Augustinus—better known as Augustine of Hippo—a man whose restless heart would find its rest not only in God but also in the sacred pursuit of wisdom.

Born in 354 AD in Thagaste, a provincial North African town under Roman rule (in modern-day Algeria), Augustine was raised in a household divided by faith. His mother, Monica, was a devout Christian who prayed fervently for his conversion; his father, Patricius, remained a pagan until his death. This tension between competing worldviews—Christian piety and classical philosophy—defined Augustine's early spiritual struggle. A brilliant student trained in rhetoric and literature, Augustine pursued education with ambition, seeking both social advancement and philosophical clarity.

But clarity eluded him. He joined the Manichaeans, a dualistic sect promising cosmic explanations for the problem of evil, only to find their doctrines shallow. He then turned to Neoplatonism, where he encountered a more refined philosophical system rooted in the teachings of Plotinus.

Though Neoplatonism elevated his understanding of immaterial realities and the soul's ascent to the divine, it still left his heart unsatisfied. He remained caught between the love of wisdom and the absence of grace.

Augustine's decisive turning point came not in a lecture hall but in a garden, in a moment of anguish and divine invitation. As he recounts in his *Confessions,* he heard a child's voice repeating the words *Tolle lege*—"Take and read." Opening the Scriptures to Romans 13, Augustine was struck by the call to abandon sin and be clothed in Christ. This conversion moment was not simply an emotional awakening; it was an intellectual and spiritual reorientation. For Augustine, the divide between mind and soul dissolved—learning and loving, reason and faith, were no longer adversaries. They were, in fact, inseparable allies in the pursuit of God.

Following his conversion, Augustine was baptized by Ambrose of Milan and eventually became the Bishop of Hippo. From this position, Augustine preached and wrote with profound theological depth, leaving behind a legacy of works that continue to shape Christian thought and practice. His writings—Confessions, The City of God, and On Christian Doctrine—established a theological framework that integrated faith and reason, challenging both ancient philosophical assumptions and contemporary Christian misunderstandings. But more than anything, Augustine left the Church with a vision of the intellectual life as a sacred vocation. He insisted that to think deeply is to pray faithfully, and to study wisely is to worship truly. For Augustine, the mind was not a hindrance to holiness—it was the pathway to behold the beauty of God.

Learning as a Sacred Act

One of Augustine's most profound theological insights was his view of learning as a sacred endeavor. In a theological climate where reason and faith were often viewed as opposing forces, Augustine insisted that intellectual pursuit was not merely compatible with faith—it was a form of devotion to God. To seek knowledge was to seek God's truth, and to understand creation was to encounter the Creator's order and wisdom.

For Augustine, learning was not a secular task but a sacred one. He argued that the mind itself is a gift from God and that the pursuit of knowledge is an act of stewardship over that gift. Augustine's view of education as a spiritual discipline is reflected in his distinction between scientia (knowledge of temporal things) and sapientia (knowledge of eternal things). According to Augustine, scientia is valuable because it equips believers to live wisely in the present world. However, sapientia is superior because it directs the soul toward eternal truths and union with God.

This view of learning as a sacred act extended beyond theological study. Scholars such as Lee and Ko have pointed out that Augustine saw the study of the liberal arts as an opportunity to uncover the "order of things" and thereby perceive the wisdom of God in creation.[5] Mathematics, astronomy, music, and rhetoric were not merely secular disciplines—they were pathways toward understanding God's created order. Academic work, therefore, was not a means of intellectual self-promotion but a contemplative act that directed the mind and heart toward God.

Charry emphasizes that Augustine's approach to learning was fundamentally transformational.[6] For Augustine, knowledge was incomplete unless it led the heart toward greater love for God. Education was not simply about acquiring information—it was about formation. The goal of intellectual work was not only understanding but worship.[7] This challenges modern distinctions between academic study and spiritual formation, inviting believers to see the life of the mind as an essential component of discipleship.

Divine Illumination: Knowing by Grace

Central to Augustine's understanding of learning is the concept of divine illumination. While Augustine valued intellectual rigor, he recognized that human reason alone was insufficient for grasping eternal truth. He believed

---

[5] Lee and Ko, "From Rational Inquiry," 122.

[6] Charry, "Educating for Wisdom," 295–308.

[7] Charry, "Educating for Wisdom," 295–308.

that human understanding was darkened by sin and that the mind's capacity to comprehend truth was ultimately dependent upon divine grace.

Augustine's doctrine of illumination teaches that true understanding comes when God enlightens the human mind. Just as physical sight depends on the presence of light, intellectual sight depends on the light of divine grace. Reason, for Augustine, is not autonomous—it is dependent. Human beings can investigate the truths of creation and Scripture, but ultimate understanding comes only when God illuminates the mind.

This view challenges both the rationalist assumption that reason alone can arrive at truth and the anti-intellectual tendency to devalue reason in favor of emotional or spiritual experience. Augustine's doctrine of illumination positions learning as an act of humility. The scholar must seek not only knowledge but also grace. As Augustine writes in *Confessions*, "Late have I loved you, beauty so ancient and so new... You called and shouted and burst my deafness; you flashed, shone, and scattered my blindness."[8] Augustine's intellectual and spiritual awakening was not the product of philosophical inquiry alone—it was the result of God's gracious illumination.

Lee and Ko underscore that this dependence on divine illumination elevates the act of learning into an act of worship. Intellectual achievement is not an occasion for pride but for reverence.[9] The mind's capacity to grasp truth is not a mark of human greatness but of God's generosity. This theological vision transforms the classroom into a sanctuary and the academic task into an act of devotion.[10]

Knowledge as a Path to Love

For Augustine, the ultimate purpose of learning is not knowledge but love. Intellectual pursuit, if it does not lead to greater love for God and neighbor, is incomplete. This is where Augustine's distinction between scientia and

---

[8] Augustine, *Confessions*, 10.27.38

[9] Lee and Ko, "From Rational Inquiry," 122.

[10] Charry, "Educating for Wisdom," 295–308.

sapientia becomes most relevant. Scientia, the knowledge of earthly things, is valuable, but it must ultimately be directed toward sapientia—the knowledge of God and eternal things.[11] When human learning becomes disconnected from divine wisdom, it degenerates into arrogance and vanity. But when human knowledge is illuminated by divine grace, it becomes a means of loving God more deeply.

Charry points out that this is why Augustine saw intellectual work as a moral exercise. The scholar's task is not merely to master information but to cultivate humility and love.[12] Pride in knowledge leads to spiritual blindness, while humility in learning leads to deeper wisdom. The true scholar, according to Augustine, is one who seeks knowledge not to elevate themselves but to love God and serve others.

This challenges modern academic culture, which often prizes intellectual accomplishment as an end in itself. Augustine's vision of education calls believers to see learning not as a means of personal advancement but as a form of spiritual formation. The intellectual life is not a competition—it is a pilgrimage toward God.

Learning as Worship

Augustine's view of learning as the pursuit of God challenges contemporary Christian attitudes toward education. Too often, the church has treated academic study and spiritual devotion as separate spheres of life. Intellectual rigor has been viewed with suspicion, while emotional experience has been prized as the true measure of faith. Augustine's vision, however, refuses this false dichotomy.

Learning, for Augustine, is an act of worship. When the mind engages with truth, the heart is drawn toward the Creator. When the believer studies the order of creation, they perceive the wisdom of God's hand. The classroom becomes a sacred space where human reason and divine grace intersect.

---

[11] Charry, "Educating for Wisdom," 295–308.

[12] Charry, "Educating for Wisdom," 295–308.

For Pentecostals, Augustine's vision offers a corrective to the tendency to separate spiritual experience from intellectual formation. Just as charismatic worship engages the heart and spirit, theological study engages the mind and understanding. True Pentecostal worship is not diminished by intellectual engagement—it is deepened by it. To pray with the spirit and with understanding means to worship with both heart and mind fully engaged. Augustine's model invites Pentecostals to recover the life of the mind as an essential component of spiritual formation.

Reflection Questions

1. How does Augustine's integration of faith and reason challenge your current understanding of worship and learning?
2. In what ways does the concept of divine illumination reshape the way you approach theological study and reflection?
3. How can Pentecostal churches cultivate a deeper commitment to both spiritual experience and intellectual rigor?
4. How does the distinction between scientia and sapientia apply to your own pursuit of knowledge and faith?
5. In what ways can learning become an act of worship in your personal and communal life?

4

Uniting Faith and Reason

The 13th century was a period of dramatic intellectual renewal in Western Europe. The rediscovery of Aristotle's writings, translated from Arabic and Greek sources, sparked a theological and philosophical revolution. As these texts filtered into European universities, they introduced a rigorous new approach to knowledge—one rooted in empirical observation, systematic logic, and the exploration of causality. The rise of scholasticism reflected a growing belief that human reason could be used not only to understand the natural world but to explore divine mysteries. But this also raised deep theological concerns. Could reason be trusted to approach the sacred? Was philosophical inquiry a friend or foe to revealed truth?

Amid these questions, one figure emerged whose work would transform the landscape of Christian theology: Thomas Aquinas. A Dominican friar born into nobility in Roccasecca, Italy, Aquinas defied his family's expectations by choosing a life of religious devotion and scholarly pursuit. His entry into the Dominican Order placed him at the heart of a movement committed to preaching, study, and poverty—ideals that shaped his life's work. He studied under Albertus Magnus, absorbed the intellectual currents of Paris and Cologne, and undertook a bold theological project: to reconcile the newly recovered philosophy of Aristotle with the faith of the Church.

Aquinas's approach was both daring and deeply reverent. At a time when many viewed Aristotelian reason with suspicion, Aquinas insisted that all truth—whether discovered by faith or by reason—had its origin in God. His magnum opus, *Summa Theologica*, was not a cold academic text but a devotional act of synthesis, a cathedral of thought built to glorify the Creator. It spanned theology, philosophy, ethics, and metaphysics, all shaped by the conviction that the mind itself is a gift from God, and to use it rightly is to worship rightly.

Yet Aquinas was not only a scholar. He was a mystic and a man of prayer. Toward the end of his life, after a profound vision during Mass, he laid down his pen and declared that all he had written was as straw compared to what had been revealed to him directly by God. In this paradox—of immense intellectual rigor paired with spiritual humility—we find the heart of Aquinas's legacy. He did not pit faith against reason, nor did he reduce theology to mere logic. Instead, he showed that the search for understanding could itself be an act of devotion, and that the mind, like the soul, must be offered wholly to God.

Faith and Reason as Complementary Truths

Aquinas's most enduring contribution to Christian thought lies in his synthesis of faith and reason. In a theological environment where reason was often viewed with suspicion and faith was positioned as a mystical alternative to intellectual inquiry, Aquinas proposed that the two realms were not in conflict but were mutually reinforcing. Faith and reason, according to Aquinas, both originate from God. Since God is the source of all truth, truths discovered through reason in the natural world cannot contradict truths revealed through faith.[13]

This conviction is most fully articulated in *Summa Theologica*, where Aquinas draws on Aristotelian logic and metaphysics to examine the nature of God, creation, morality, and salvation. For Aquinas, the natural world is intelligible because it reflects the order and wisdom of its Creator. Human reason, as a reflection of the imago Dei (the image of God), is capable of

---

[13] Elders, "Aristotelian Commentaries," 29–53.

discerning this order. Therefore, intellectual inquiry is not merely a human activity—it is a sacred endeavor that participates in God's creative wisdom.

Leo Elders emphasizes that Aquinas viewed nature as God's art, directed toward specific ends.[14] This teleological view of creation shaped Aquinas's understanding of reason and knowledge. Thinking, for Aquinas, is not merely a mental exercise—it is a form of worship.[15] When human beings use their rational faculties to uncover the order of creation, they are participating in God's divine plan. Learning and philosophical reflection become acts of devotion, whereby the mind reflects the wisdom of its Creator.

This connection between faith and reason is crucial for understanding Aquinas's broader theological vision. According to Roberto Di Ceglie, Aquinas trusted human reason precisely because it comes from God.[16] If human reason is a gift from God, then it cannot ultimately lead people away from God. The pursuit of knowledge is not an act of intellectual arrogance but an act of obedience and reverence. When believers seek to understand the natural world or explore theological questions, they are not setting faith aside—they are honoring God with their minds.

Kevin O'Reilly highlights how Aquinas's framework establishes a clear path from intellectual inquiry to spiritual fulfillment.[17] The human mind, when properly ordered, leads to God. To know truth is to know God, because God is the source and fullness of all truth. Intellectual activity, therefore, becomes a spiritual discipline—an exercise in learning to think God's thoughts after Him. In this way, Aquinas transforms learning into an act of worship.

The Imago Dei and the Intellectual Life

At the core of Aquinas's integration of faith and reason is the concept of the imago Dei. Aquinas taught that human beings are created in the image of God,

---

14 Elders, "Aristotelian Commentaries," 29–53.

15 O'Reilly, "Significance of Worship," 453–62.

16 Di Ceglie, "Sacrificial View of Life," 876.

17 O'Reilly, "Significance of Worship," 453–62.

which includes the capacity for rational thought and moral discernment.[18] This intellectual capacity is not an accidental feature of human nature—it is a reflection of God's own wisdom.

This understanding of the human mind as a reflection of divine intelligence means that intellectual activity is fundamentally sacred. Aquinas believed that the human mind's capacity to reason was a participation in God's wisdom. Therefore, to engage in philosophical or scientific inquiry is to exercise a faculty that points toward God.

Aquinas's doctrine of the imago Dei also establishes the moral significance of intellectual humility. If human reason is a gift from God, then intellectual achievement is not a basis for pride but for gratitude and reverence. This perspective challenges both intellectual arrogance and anti-intellectualism. The true scholar, according to Aquinas, is not one who seeks knowledge for self-glorification but one who seeks to glorify God through the use of reason.

Furthermore, Aquinas's view of the imago Dei presents a theological foundation for the unity of all knowledge. Since truth originates from God, all fields of knowledge—whether theological, philosophical, or scientific—are ultimately part of a single intellectual order. This challenges the modern tendency to separate sacred and secular knowledge. For Aquinas, all truth is God's truth, and the intellectual life is an integrated whole that reflects the unity of divine wisdom.

Learning as Worship

Aquinas's synthesis of faith and reason offers a profound theological foundation for understanding learning as an act of worship. Learning, for Aquinas, is not simply about mastering facts or acquiring knowledge. It is about participating in God's truth and discovering the divine order embedded in creation. To study the natural world is to encounter the wisdom of the Creator; to reflect on theological truth is to draw near to God.[19]

---

[18] Aquinas, *Summa Theologica* I q.93 a.4.

[19] Elders, "Aristotelian Commentaries," 29–53.

This perspective challenges the modern division between academic and spiritual life. In many contemporary contexts, intellectual activity is treated as a secular task, while spiritual devotion is confined to prayer and worship. Aquinas's vision, however, recognizes no such division. The life of the mind and the life of faith are two sides of the same coin. To think deeply about God is to worship Him; to understand the order of creation is to glimpse His wisdom.

This is why Aquinas viewed theological study as a sacred task. The work of the scholar is not separate from the work of the church—it is an extension of it. Theologians and philosophers are not merely academic specialists; they are servants of the truth, tasked with leading others into a deeper understanding of God's revelation. The intellectual life, rightly ordered, is a form of worship that reflects the glory of God's truth.

Faith Seeking Understanding

Aquinas's model of faith and reason invites contemporary Pentecostals to rethink the role of intellectual formation in spiritual life. Pentecostal spirituality often emphasizes the immediacy of the Spirit's presence and the power of direct encounter with God. But Aquinas's teaching suggests that intellectual formation and spiritual encounter are not opposing forces—they are complementary.[20]

To engage the mind in theological reflection is not to diminish the Spirit's work—it is to deepen it. The same Spirit who inspires prophecy and prayer also inspires understanding and wisdom. True Pentecostal worship should engage both the spirit and the mind, the heart and the intellect. The intellectual life, when rightly ordered, becomes a pathway to greater intimacy with God.

Aquinas's vision challenges Pentecostals to embrace theological reflection as an essential part of discipleship. Faith seeking understanding is not an academic exercise—it is an act of worship. Learning to think about God

---

[20] O'Reilly, "Significance of Worship," 453–62.

rightly is part of learning to love Him fully. The integration of faith and reason is not an intellectual achievement—it is a spiritual calling.

Reflection Questions

1. How does Aquinas's synthesis of faith and reason challenge your current understanding of worship and theological reflection?
2. How does the concept of the imago Dei shape your view of human reason and intellectual capacity?
3. In what ways can Pentecostal churches promote both charismatic experience and intellectual depth in worship?
4. How can the pursuit of knowledge become an act of devotion in your personal and communal life?
5. How does Aquinas's view of reason and faith shape your approach to Scripture and theological study?

5

"Education is Killing Christianity"

The dawn of the twentieth century witnessed a spiritual eruption that would reshape the face of global Christianity. In a modest, weatherworn building at 312 Azusa Street in Los Angeles, people from diverse racial and social backgrounds gathered to seek a fresh move of God. What happened there in 1906 would come to be known as the Azusa Street Revival—an uncontainable outpouring of the Holy Spirit marked by speaking in tongues, prophetic visions, miraculous healings, and ecstatic worship. The revival, led by the African-American preacher William J. Seymour, ignited the modern Pentecostal movement—a movement that would grow to become one of the most vibrant and fastest-growing expressions of Christianity in the world.[21]

Yet from its very beginning, Pentecostalism bore the marks of an uneasy relationship with the life of the mind. The early movement was born among the marginalized—poor, Black, immigrant, and working-class believers who had long been excluded from the theological and academic halls of power. The Holy Spirit's descent at Azusa Street bypassed the seminaries and universities, arriving instead in a humble prayer meeting filled with spiritual hunger. This spiritual democracy fueled the conviction that academic credentials were unnecessary for divine empowerment. What mattered most was not theological pedigree, but spiritual receptivity.

---

[21] Nel, "Development of Theological Training and Hermeneutics."

This conviction, however, quickly gave way to something more severe: a suspicion, even a rejection, of formal education. The roots of this anti-intellectualism ran deep. William J. Seymour had been a student of Charles Fox Parham, who founded the Bethel Bible School in Topeka, Kansas.[22] Parham's vision of biblical training was deliberately simple—tuition-free, relying solely on the Bible, with no reliance on tradition, philosophy, or theology. Parham believed that spiritual insight was received directly from the Holy Spirit, not through the careful exegesis of Scripture or the long arc of church history. His disdain for intellectual formation became a defining feature of early Pentecostal identity.[23]

At Azusa Street, this suspicion toward education became woven into the fabric of revival life. Services were spontaneous, marked by tongues, trances, and trembling. There was no formal liturgy, no systematic theology, no structured teaching. Theological reflection was seen as suspect—something cold and lifeless, a threat to the living fire of the Spirit. The testimonies that filled the pages of *The Apostolic Faith*, the revival's main publication, often warned readers against Intellectualism. One early Pentecostal was even quoted as saying that "education is killing Christianity."[24] In the eyes of many early Pentecostals, the academy had failed to produce revival, while uneducated believers tarried in prayer and received the power of God.

But this early anti-intellectualism came at a cost. By dismissing the role of theological reflection, Pentecostalism severed itself from the deep wells of Christian tradition and left itself vulnerable to doctrinal instability. What began as a Spirit-led revival became, in some quarters, an anti-intellectual reaction. The same fire that fell at Azusa illuminated hearts but left the mind in shadow. To reclaim the full inheritance of Pentecostal faith, the movement must revisit its origins—not to abandon the Spirit, but to rediscover how the mind too may burn with holy fire.

---

[22] Nanez, *Full Gospel, Fractured Minds?*.

[23] GotQuestions.org, "Who Was Charles Parham?"

[24] Nanez, *Full Gospel, Fractured Minds?*.

The Apostolic Faith and the Rejection of Intellectualism

The anti-intellectual spirit of early Pentecostalism was widely disseminated through The Apostolic Faith, the main publication of the Azusa Street Revival.[25] The Apostolic Faith consistently presented theological reflection and academic study as obstacles to true faith. The publication framed spiritual hunger and intellectual engagement as mutually exclusive. As Rick M. Nanez summarizes, The Apostolic Faith repeatedly asserted that "the truly hungry were being touched by the Spirit, while thinkers and theologians refused him." This reflected a broader Pentecostal tendency to equate intellectual humility with suspicion toward academic inquiry.

For early Pentecostals, the rejection of theological reflection was not merely practical—it was theological. To seek knowledge through study was viewed as a form of human striving, a distraction from the immediacy of the Spirit's work. True knowledge, according to early Pentecostals, was not gained through systematic reflection but through spiritual experience. The experience of the Spirit—manifested in speaking in tongues, prophecy, and other charismatic gifts—was held as the highest form of revelation.

This emphasis on spiritual immediacy over theological reflection created a sharp divide between faith and reason. Pentecostal spirituality became synonymous with non-cognitive experience—feeling the Spirit, receiving visions, and speaking in tongues—while intellectual engagement was associated with spiritual deadness. The dichotomy between the heart and the mind became deeply entrenched within Pentecostal identity.

Kenneth Copeland, a prominent figure in the Word of Faith movement—a theological descendant of early Pentecostalism—embodies this anti-intellectual legacy. Copeland once declared, "Believers are not supposed to be led by logic. We are not ever to be led by good sense. The ministry of Jesus was never governed by logic or reason."[26] This statement reflects the enduring suspicion toward rational inquiry within Pentecostal culture. To

---

[25] Nanez, *Full Gospel, Fractured Minds?*.

[26] Nanez, *Full Gospel, Fractured Minds?*.

rely on reason was to risk spiritual compromise.

This legacy of anti-intellectualism has left Pentecostalism vulnerable in several key areas. The lack of theological depth has made Pentecostals susceptible to doctrinal error, manipulation, and theological instability. The reluctance to engage with broader intellectual currents has isolated Pentecostal communities from meaningful cultural and social dialogue. Without a framework for theological reflection, Pentecostals have often lacked the tools to respond to complex moral and ethical challenges.

The Costs of Anti-Intellectualism

The consequences of Pentecostal anti-intellectualism have been far-reaching. First, the lack of theological grounding has resulted in doctrinal instability within Pentecostalism. Without a coherent theological framework, Pentecostals have struggled to articulate their faith in the face of theological pluralism and secular criticism. This has led to the proliferation of prosperity theology, exaggerated claims of spiritual authority, and doctrinal confusion.

Second, the rejection of intellectual engagement has isolated Pentecostalism from the broader Christian tradition. Pentecostals have often positioned themselves in opposition to historical Christian orthodoxy, favoring experiential authenticity over doctrinal consistency. This has weakened ecumenical relationships and limited Pentecostal influence within the broader Christian community.

Third, the lack of intellectual formation has left Pentecostals poorly equipped to engage with the broader culture. In a rapidly secularizing world, where moral and philosophical challenges are increasingly complex, Pentecostals have often been relegated to the margins of intellectual discourse. The absence of a robust theological framework has made it difficult for Pentecostals to articulate a coherent social and ethical vision.

Finally, the suspicion toward reason has created an internal division within Pentecostalism itself. As Pentecostals have become more diverse and globally connected, tensions have emerged between those who emphasize charismatic experience and those who seek to develop a more intellectually engaged faith.

This divide threatens the unity and identity of the Pentecostal movement.

A Pentecostal Life of the Mind

Despite this legacy of anti-intellectualism, a growing movement within Pentecostalism is calling for the recovery of the intellectual life as an essential part of spiritual formation. Leading scholars such as Rick M. Nanez, Richard J. Mouw, James W. Sire, Amos Yong, and Dale M. Coulter have argued that intellectual engagement is not a threat to spirituality—it is a fulfillment of it.

Amos Yong has been at the forefront of this effort, calling for a "Pentecostal theology of the mind" that integrates charismatic experience with theological reflection. Yong argues that the Holy Spirit, who inspires prophetic utterance and miraculous healing, also inspires theological insight and intellectual discernment. For Yong, the intellectual life is not opposed to spiritual experience—it is an extension of it.[27]

Rick M. Nanez likewise challenges the false dichotomy between reason and faith. He contends that Pentecostals should see theological reflection as a form of worship. Studying Scripture, engaging with church history, and exploring philosophical questions are not distractions from spiritual life—they are part of it.[28]

Richard J. Mouw and James W. Sire, although not Pentecostal themselves, emphasize the importance of intellectual humility. They argue that believers must recover the historic Christian understanding of the mind as a gift from God. Intellectual formation, when rooted in humility and reverence, becomes a means of glorifying God and strengthening the church.[29]

Dale M. Coulter has worked to recover the scholastic tradition within Pentecostalism, arguing that Pentecostal spirituality must be grounded in theological depth. Coulter calls for the development of Pentecostal educational institutions that combine charismatic experience with rigorous

---

[27] Yong and Coulter, *Holy Spirit and Higher Education.*

[28] Nanez, *Full Gospel, Fractured Minds?.*

[29] Mouw, *Called to the Life of the Mind..*; Sire, *Habits of the Mind.*

theological training.[30]

This emerging movement represents a significant shift in Pentecostal identity. For the first time, Pentecostals are reclaiming the intellectual life as a distinctive charism of the Holy Spirit. The integration of reason and faith is not a betrayal of Pentecostal identity—it is a recovery of its fullness.

Reclaiming the Life of the Mind

The future of Pentecostalism may depend on its ability to overcome its anti-intellectual legacy. The Pentecostal movement cannot afford to remain intellectually disengaged in an increasingly complex and secular world. The same Spirit who inspires tongues and prophecy also inspires wisdom and understanding. Pentecostalism must reclaim the life of the mind as an act of devotion, recognizing that the pursuit of truth is itself a form of worship.

The challenge for Pentecostals today is not to choose between faith and reason but to integrate them. To worship God fully means to engage both the heart and the mind, both spiritual experience and theological reflection. A mature Pentecostal faith will pray with the spirit and with the understanding, seeking not only emotional intimacy with God but intellectual depth in knowing Him.

Reflection Questions

1. How has Pentecostal anti-intellectualism shaped your understanding of faith and learning?
2. In what ways can Pentecostal churches recover the life of the mind without losing their charismatic identity?
3. How can theological study become an act of worship in your personal life?
4. How might reclaiming intellectual engagement strengthen Pentecostal witness to the broader culture?

---

[30] Yong and Coulter, *Holy Spirit and Higher Education.*

5. How can the work of Yong, Mouw, Sire, and Coulter inform Pentecostal theological formation today?

6

Nañez: Integrating Doctrine and Experience

By the late twentieth century, Pentecostalism had become a global force—expanding into every continent, transforming worship practices, and reshaping the religious landscape of the modern world. Yet within this remarkable growth, a persistent tension lingered at the heart of the movement. Beneath the exuberance of revival and the passion of charismatic expression was an intellectual vacuum—a legacy inherited from its earliest revivalist roots. Pentecostalism, for all its vitality, had often nurtured suspicion toward theological depth and academic formation. For many Pentecostals, spiritual power and doctrinal reflection were perceived as incompatible, if not opposing, forces.

This historical tension is the focus of Rick M. Nañez's critique in *Full Gospel, Fractured Minds?*, where he explores the roots and consequences of Pentecostal anti-intellectualism.[31] Nañez does not write as a critic from the outside but as a sympathetic voice within the tradition—a Pentecostal deeply committed to the renewal of the movement's theological imagination. He traces the problem back to 19th-century revivalism, where emotional fervor was elevated and theological education was often dismissed as a barrier

---

[31] Nanez, *Full Gospel, Fractured Minds?*.

to true spiritual power.[32] This revivalist ethos shaped the DNA of early Pentecostalism, embedding a deep skepticism of the academy and an over-reliance on personal experience.

What emerged was a form of Christianity rich in affective intensity but thin in doctrinal coherence. Emotional encounters with the Spirit became the measure of authenticity, while systematic theology and biblical exegesis were sidelined. Camp meetings replaced catechesis; testimonies replaced theological training. The result was a movement ablaze with passion—but often vulnerable to theological error, spiritual instability, and cultural disengagement.

Nañez enters this historical moment with a call to rediscover the Pentecostal life of the mind—not as a betrayal of charismatic identity, but as its rightful maturation. He does not seek to extinguish the fire of revival; he seeks to channel it through thoughtful reflection. For Nañez, worship must engage not only the spirit but also the understanding. The mind, like the heart, must be set aflame by the Spirit of God.[33]

The Imbalance Between Emotion and Understanding

Nañez critiques the imbalance between emotional expression and theological understanding within Pentecostal worship. He notes that many Pentecostal churches continue to emphasize spontaneous, emotionally charged worship experiences at the expense of theological reflection. Speaking in tongues, prophetic utterances, and healing services often take center stage, while systematic teaching and biblical exposition are marginalized. The emotional intensity of Pentecostal worship creates a powerful sense of divine presence, but this experience is often left unexamined and unreflected upon.

This imbalance creates two significant problems. First, it leads to theological shallowness. Without intellectual formation, Pentecostals struggle to develop a coherent understanding of their faith. Worship becomes an

---

[32] Nanez, *Full Gospel, Fractured Minds?*.

[33] Nanez, *Full Gospel, Fractured Minds?*.

event rather than a transformative encounter with God. Pentecostals may experience powerful manifestations of the Spirit but remain theologically underdeveloped, unable to articulate the doctrinal foundations of their faith.

Second, it leads to spiritual instability. When worship is primarily emotional, it becomes difficult for believers to maintain spiritual consistency in the absence of strong emotional experiences. Faith becomes dependent on emotional highs rather than sustained theological understanding. This emotionalism leaves believers vulnerable to spiritual burnout and manipulation.

Nañez argues that Pentecostalism's historical rejection of theological depth has created a fragile spirituality—one that is easily swayed by emotional appeal but lacks the stability and resilience that comes from doctrinal formation. Pentecostals, according to Nañez, have cultivated passionate hearts but neglected thoughtful minds.[34] This imbalance has left Pentecostalism theologically underprepared to engage with complex moral, social, and philosophical challenges in the modern world.

The Need for Holistic Worship

In response to this imbalance, Nañez calls for a reimagining of Pentecostal worship as a holistic engagement of both heart and mind.[35] He insists that true worship must engage the whole person—emotions, intellect, spirit, and body. Worship that is purely emotional risks becoming shallow and unsustainable, while worship that is purely intellectual lacks the relational and experiential connection that defines Pentecostal spirituality. A balanced, holistic worship model values both theological reflection and spiritual passion.

Nañez's framework echoes the Great Commandment, where Jesus calls believers to love God with all their heart, soul, mind, and strength (Mark 12:30). Pentecostals have historically excelled at loving God with their heart and strength—expressing worship through emotional and physical manifestations. But Nañez argues that the mind and the intellect must also

---

[34] Nanez, *Full Gospel, Fractured Minds?*.

[35] Nanez, *Full Gospel, Fractured Minds?*.

be engaged. To love God with the mind means to study Scripture deeply, to engage with Christian history and doctrine, and to reflect theologically on the work of the Spirit in the church and the world.[36]

This integrated approach to worship challenges Pentecostals to move beyond the false dichotomy between spirit and understanding. Pentecostal worship can be both ecstatic and thoughtful, both spontaneous and reflective. Emotional fervor and theological depth are not opposing forces—they are complementary dimensions of human devotion. True worship engages the whole person, drawing together spiritual experience and intellectual reflection into a single act of devotion.

Nañez suggests that Pentecostal churches must create spaces for both charismatic expression and theological teaching.[37] Worship services should incorporate both spontaneous movements of the Spirit and structured teaching of the Word. Prophetic utterance should be accompanied by careful discernment; speaking in tongues should be balanced with theological interpretation. Nañez's vision for Pentecostal worship is not less charismatic—it is more theologically aware and spiritually mature.

Doctrine as an Act of Worship

Nañez emphasizes that engaging the mind in theological reflection is itself an act of worship. Pentecostals often associate worship with emotional expression—singing, shouting, and spontaneous prayer—but Nañez argues that studying Scripture, reflecting on doctrine, and engaging with theological questions are also forms of worship.[38] To think deeply about God is to glorify Him with the gift of intellect.

This understanding transforms the academic task into a spiritual discipline. Pentecostals have often viewed theological study as a dry and lifeless activity, disconnected from the immediacy of spiritual encounter. But Nañez contends

---

[36] Nanez, *Full Gospel, Fractured Minds?*.

[37] Nanez, *Full Gospel, Fractured Minds?*.

[38] Nanez, *Full Gospel, Fractured Minds?*.

that theological reflection is not an intellectual distraction from faith—it is a deepening of it. To seek understanding is to seek God; to know truth is to know Christ.[39]

Engaging with doctrine also equips Pentecostals for faithful witness in the world. A mature faith requires both spiritual passion and intellectual depth. The ability to engage with contemporary moral and social issues requires theological formation. Pentecostals who are deeply rooted in Scripture and Christian tradition will be better equipped to respond to ethical complexity, cultural challenges, and interfaith dialogue. Nañez calls Pentecostals to become thoughtful theologians without losing the charismatic vitality that defines their spiritual identity.[40]

Maturity Through Integration

Nañez argues that spiritual maturity comes through the integration of doctrine and experience.[41] Pentecostal worship that engages both the heart and the mind produces believers who are emotionally authentic and intellectually grounded. This balance creates a stable and resilient faith—one that can withstand emotional highs and lows because it is rooted in theological depth.

Nañez points to biblical figures such as the Apostle Paul as models of this integration.[42] Paul was both a charismatic leader and a rigorous theologian. He spoke in tongues and exercised the gifts of the Spirit, but he also wrote deeply theological letters that have shaped Christian doctrine for centuries. For Nañez, Paul represents the ideal Pentecostal leader—a figure who combines spiritual passion with intellectual depth.[43]

This integration, Nañez argues, will not weaken Pentecostal identity—it will

---

[39] Nanez, *Full Gospel, Fractured Minds?*.

[40] Nanez, *Full Gospel, Fractured Minds?*.

[41] Nanez, *Full Gospel, Fractured Minds?*.

[42] Nanez, *Full Gospel, Fractured Minds?*.

[43] Nanez, *Full Gospel, Fractured Minds?*.

strengthen it. A [44]Pentecostalism that is both charismatic and theologically mature will be better equipped to engage with the broader church and the contemporary world. Nañez envisions a Pentecostal movement that maintains its distinctive emphasis on the Spirit's work while embracing theological formation as a vital dimension of spiritual life.[45]

This vision challenges Pentecostals to reclaim the intellectual life as an essential part of their identity. The future of Pentecostalism lies not in choosing between emotional experience and theological reflection but in embracing both as essential expressions of worship. A mature Pentecostal faith will be one that prays with the spirit and the understanding—a faith that sings with the heart and reflects with the mind.

Reflection Questions

1. How has Pentecostalism's historical resistance to intellectual engagement shaped your understanding of faith and worship?
2. In what ways can Pentecostal churches create more space for theological reflection while maintaining charismatic expression?
3. How can studying doctrine and engaging in theological reflection become an act of worship in your own life?
4. How does Nañez's call to balance heart and mind reshape your view of Pentecostal worship?
5. How can the integration of doctrine and experience strengthen Pentecostal witness in a complex cultural landscape?

---

[44] Nañez, *Full Gospel, Fractured Minds?*.

[45] Nañez, *Full Gospel, Fractured Minds?*.

7

Mouw: Worship as Intellectual Devotion

In the shifting landscape of modern Christianity, few voices have spoken more clearly about the relationship between faith and reason than Richard J. Mouw.[46] A philosopher by training and a theologian by calling, Mouw has long stood at the intersection of evangelical faith and intellectual inquiry, urging the Church to reject the false choice between heartfelt worship and thoughtful reflection. In a religious culture often shaped by revivalism and emotional immediacy, Mouw's voice rings with a different timbre—one that invites believers to see the life of the mind not as a threat to spiritual vitality, but as an act of devotion in its own right.

Mouw came of age in the latter half of the twentieth century, when evangelicalism was grappling with the twin forces of cultural relevance and theological depth. The church had emerged from the shadows of the fundamentalist-modernist debates with a renewed emphasis on personal conversion and biblical fidelity, yet often retained a latent suspicion toward intellectual complexity.[47] For Pentecostals and other charismatic traditions, this suspicion was magnified by a historic prioritization of experience—especially the spontaneous and emotional manifestations of the Holy Spirit. In this environment, worship was often equated with feeling, and intellectual

---

[46] Mouw, *Called to the Life of the Mind.*

[47] Nañez, *Full Gospel, Fractured Minds?.*

engagement was relegated to the margins.

Mouw offers a different path. Grounded in the Reformed tradition yet deeply respectful of charismatic spirituality, he articulates a vision of worship that embraces the full range of human faculties. For Mouw, to think deeply is not to stray from God, but to move closer to Him. The mind, he insists, is not the enemy of the Spirit—it is His ally. Drawing from the biblical command to love God with all one's heart, soul, and mind, Mouw contends that intellectual activity is not merely a preparation for worship—it *is* worship. In a time when many churches fear that complexity will quench the Spirit, Mouw's theology declares that the pursuit of understanding may in fact fan the flames of devotion.[48]

This vision is particularly pressing for us as Pentecostals. Our worship is known for its spiritual fervor but our intellectual tradition remains underdeveloped. Mouw's theological imagination calls Pentecostals to reclaim the mind as a sacred vessel—to see theology not as a cold abstraction but as a form of love, a way of thinking about God that is itself animated by the Spirit. In doing so, Mouw invites a new kind of Pentecostalism to emerge—one that is as thoughtful as it is passionate, as doctrinally rooted as it is prophetically free.[49]

Embracing Questions and Doubts

A key element of Mouw's vision for intellectual devotion is the creation of space for questions and doubts within the life of the church. Mouw challenges the notion that theological inquiry and intellectual questioning are threats to faith. He argues that faith is not weakened by honest questions—it is strengthened by them. To seek understanding is not to doubt God's truth but to participate in the search for it.[50]

This stands in contrast to the defensive posture toward questions that has

---

[48] Mouw, *Called to the Life of the Mind.*

[49] Mouw, *Called to the Life of the Mind.*

[50] Mouw, *Called to the Life of the Mind.*

often characterized Pentecostal and revivalist traditions. In many Pentecostal settings, theological questions have been met with suspicion or outright dismissal. Believers who raise difficult questions are sometimes accused of lacking faith or spiritual maturity. The standard response to theological discomfort is often to "just have faith" or to rely on the Holy Spirit to provide understanding.

Mouw challenges this approach. He argues that God is not threatened by human inquiry.[51] If God is the source of all truth, then genuine questions—whether about Scripture, doctrine, or the nature of God—are not obstacles to faith but opportunities for deeper understanding. A church that welcomes questions is a church that trusts in the faithfulness of God to reveal Himself through Scripture, reason, and experience.

This has direct implications for Pentecostal worship. A worshiping community that embraces Mouw's framework will create environments where believers feel free to wrestle with theological questions without fear of judgment. Sermons and Bible studies will address difficult topics rather than avoid them. Doctrinal exploration will be encouraged, not discouraged. Worship services will incorporate both spontaneous spiritual expressions and structured theological teaching.

Mouw's model suggests that true Pentecostal vitality comes not from avoiding difficult questions but from engaging with them. A church that thinks deeply about God's nature and works will be a church that worships God more authentically and passionately. The Spirit is not diminished by intellectual reflection—He is revealed through it.

Worship as a Holistic Encounter

Mouw's framework ultimately calls for a holistic vision of Christian worship—one that engages the whole person. For Mouw, true worship is not limited to emotional or spiritual expressions; it encompasses intellectual engagement,

---

[51] Mouw, *Called to the Life of the Mind.*

moral reflection, and theological inquiry.[52] Worship that engages the mind deepens the emotional and spiritual dimensions of faith rather than detracting from them.

This approach aligns with the biblical model of worship. The Psalms reflect both emotional intimacy with God and thoughtful reflection on His nature and works. Jesus' teaching engages both the heart and the mind, combining moral instruction with theological depth. Paul's epistles reflect both charismatic experience and intellectual rigor. Christian worship, in its fullest expression, reflects this integrated pattern.

Mouw calls Pentecostals to embody this biblical model of holistic worship.[53] A church that sings passionately but also thinks deeply will reflect the full scope of human devotion. Worship that engages the mind will produce theological maturity; worship that engages the heart will produce spiritual intimacy. The goal is not to diminish Pentecostal distinctiveness but to deepen it—to bring Pentecostal worship into greater alignment with the biblical call to love God with all one's heart, soul, and mind.

By adopting Mouw's framework, Pentecostals can reclaim the life of the mind as a legitimate and essential aspect of faith. They can cultivate churches that are intellectually engaged and spiritually vibrant. They can foster a worshiping community where emotional fervor and theological depth reinforce rather than oppose one another. This is the vision that Mouw offers—a church where the mind and the heart unite in the pursuit of God's truth.

Intellectual Devotion and Pentecostal Identity

Mouw's vision of intellectual devotion presents an opportunity for Pentecostalism to recover its theological depth while preserving its charismatic identity. Pentecostal worship need not sacrifice emotional spontaneity for theological reflection—it can embrace both. The same Spirit who inspires

---

[52] Mouw, *Called to the Life of the Mind.*

[53] Mouw, *Called to the Life of the Mind.*

tongues and prophecy also inspires wisdom and understanding.

This integration will equip Pentecostals to engage more effectively with contemporary culture. A theologically informed Pentecostalism will be better positioned to address moral, social, and philosophical questions with credibility and coherence. The Pentecostal witness will be strengthened, not weakened, by intellectual engagement.

Ultimately, Mouw's vision points to a Pentecostal future where the church prays with the spirit and the understanding—a church that worships God with passion and with depth, with emotional authenticity and theological maturity. This is the future that Pentecostalism can—and should—embrace.

Reflection Questions

1. How does Mouw's vision for intellectual engagement challenge your understanding of Pentecostal worship?
2. In what ways can Pentecostal churches create environments where theological inquiry and emotional expression are both encouraged?
3. How can engaging the mind in theological reflection deepen your personal worship practices?
4. What steps can your church take to cultivate a more theologically informed worship experience?
5. How does the integration of heart and mind in worship reflect the biblical model of devotion?

8

Sire: Forming the Mind for Worship

In the closing decades of the twentieth century, a quiet but profound voice emerged within the evangelical world—one that called the Church to think more deeply, more carefully, and more faithfully. James W. Sire, a former editor at InterVarsity Press and a lifelong advocate for the Christian mind, challenged believers to view intellectual formation not as a luxury of the academy but as a necessity for spiritual maturity. His work was not driven by abstract curiosity, but by a deep conviction: that cultivating intellectual virtues is essential to authentic worship.

Sire's influence came at a time when much of Western Christianity had grown comfortable with anti-intellectual patterns. Emotional expression, pragmatic ministry, and experiential spirituality often displaced thoughtful engagement with theology, philosophy, and biblical interpretation. In revivalist and Pentecostal traditions especially, the life of the mind was sometimes seen as suspect—viewed as cold, lifeless, or even an impediment to the Spirit's work. But Sire believed that to think well was not to betray the faith—it was to honor it. The intellectual virtues, for Sire, were not incidental to discipleship; they were central to it.

Rather than separating the life of the mind from the life of the Spirit, Sire sought to recover an integrated vision.[54] Drawing from the deep wells

---

[54] Sire, *Habits of the Mind.*

of classical philosophy and biblical theology, he identified virtues such as humility, perseverance, and integrity as essential habits of thought that shape Christian character. These were not simply cognitive disciplines—they were spiritual dispositions. To think with humility was to acknowledge one's dependence on God. To persevere in the search for truth was to participate in the long obedience of faith. To think with integrity was to align one's knowledge with one's life. For Sire, these intellectual virtues were nothing less than acts of worship.

This vision has profound implications for Pentecostalism, where worship is often defined by charismatic encounter but rarely by intellectual discipline. Sire's theology does not diminish the fire of Pentecostal experience—it refines it. He invites Pentecostals to see that the same Spirit who moves in prophecy and healing also moves in study and reflection. The intellectual life, when shaped by virtue and directed toward God, is not a threat to Pentecostal identity. It is a pathway to its maturity.

The Virtue of Humility in Worship

Sire identifies humility as one of the foundational intellectual virtues.[55] Humility in worship means recognizing the limits of human understanding and maintaining a posture of openness toward God's truth. It involves acknowledging that God's nature and purposes exceed human comprehension and that theological reflection requires both reverence and intellectual modesty.

In a Pentecostal context, humility challenges the assumption that spiritual experience alone provides a complete understanding of God. While the immediacy of the Spirit's presence is a vital part of Pentecostal identity, it does not negate the need for theological reflection and discernment. Humility requires believers to recognize that spiritual experience must be tested and interpreted through the lens of Scripture and sound doctrine.

Humility in worship also requires a willingness to receive correction and

---

[55] Sire, *Habits of the Mind.*

instruction. Sire argues that intellectual humility involves being teachable—recognizing that one's understanding of Scripture and doctrine is always partial and subject to refinement.[56] For Pentecostals, this means being open to deeper theological formation and engaging with the broader Christian tradition. Worship that is rooted in humility becomes a space where believers are not only emotionally renewed but also intellectually challenged and refined.

This virtue challenges the tendency toward theological isolationism that has often characterized Pentecostalism. Pentecostals have sometimes resisted dialogue with other Christian traditions out of a desire to preserve their distinctive identity. Humility, as Sire defines it, calls Pentecostals to engage with the broader body of Christ in a spirit of openness and learning. Worship informed by humility reflects a willingness to learn from the wisdom of the historic church while remaining faithful to the Pentecostal emphasis on the Spirit's work.

Perseverance in the Pursuit of Truth

Perseverance, according to Sire, is the intellectual virtue that sustains the pursuit of truth through difficulty and uncertainty. [57] It reflects a commitment to theological inquiry even when answers are not immediately apparent. Perseverance requires believers to wrestle with difficult questions rather than settling for simplistic or emotionally satisfying answers.

Sire's emphasis on perseverance challenges Pentecostals to move beyond superficial understandings of Scripture and doctrine. Pentecostal worship often prizes spontaneity and immediacy—emotional encounters with God are seen as signs of spiritual authenticity. However, Sire argues that true spiritual maturity requires the discipline of sustained theological reflection. Worship is not only about immediate emotional gratification—it is about the long-term formation of the mind and spirit.

---

[56] Sire, *Habits of the Mind.*

[57] Sire, *Habits of the Mind.*

Perseverance in worship means that believers are willing to sit with unresolved questions and theological tensions. For Pentecostals, this might involve grappling with difficult doctrinal issues such as the nature of the Trinity, the role of spiritual gifts, or the relationship between faith and reason. Rather than seeking immediate resolution, perseverance calls believers to trust that deeper understanding will emerge through ongoing study and reflection.

This virtue also applies to Pentecostal preaching and teaching. Sire suggests that perseverance requires churches to commit to sustained theological instruction rather than relying solely on emotional appeal. [58] Pentecostal sermons that engage with complex theological questions and challenge believers to think deeply about their faith foster intellectual perseverance. Worship services that balance charismatic expression with structured teaching create a space where believers can grow both spiritually and intellectually.

Perseverance also applies to spiritual practice. Prayer, for example, is not always an emotionally gratifying experience. Sire argues that intellectual perseverance involves continuing to pray, study, and seek God even when emotional intensity fades. A persevering faith is one that remains committed to theological exploration and spiritual growth even in the absence of immediate emotional reward.

Integrity: Uniting Thought and Action

Integrity, for Sire, is the virtue that ensures intellectual engagement remains ethically and spiritually consistent. Integrity means that theological reflection is not merely an intellectual exercise but a foundation for moral and spiritual living. To know truth is to live truth. Integrity requires believers to align their understanding of God with their daily lives.[59]

For Pentecostals, this challenges the tendency to separate spiritual experience from moral responsibility. Pentecostal worship often emphasizes divine

---

[58] Sire, *Habits of the Mind.*

[59] Sire, *Habits of the Mind.*

encounter and personal renewal, but Sire argues that true worship requires ethical consistency. Speaking in tongues, prophecy, and healing must be accompanied by a commitment to justice, compassion, and moral integrity.

Integrity in worship also demands authenticity. Sire critiques the tendency within some Pentecostal circles to measure spiritual authenticity by emotional intensity alone.[60] Integrity means that worship is not about performance or emotional manipulation—it is about aligning the heart, mind, and will with God's truth. Authentic worship reflects not only emotional sincerity but also theological accuracy and moral responsibility.

Integrity also challenges Pentecostals to engage with the broader social and cultural issues of their time. A church that worships with integrity cannot remain silent on issues of justice, human dignity, and moral responsibility. Integrity requires that theological reflection shapes ethical action. For Pentecostals, this means applying biblical truth to contemporary challenges such as racial reconciliation, economic justice, and political engagement.

Worship that reflects integrity creates a space where believers are not only emotionally renewed but also morally transformed. Sire's vision calls Pentecostals to see worship as a formative practice that shapes both individual character and communal identity. A church that worships with integrity becomes a credible witness to the broader culture—a community whose theological depth and moral consistency reflect the truth of the gospel.[61]

Cultivating Intellectual Virtues in Pentecostal Worship

Sire offers practical strategies for cultivating intellectual virtues within Pentecostal worship. First, he calls for the creation of spaces for theological inquiry and dialogue within the church.[62] Pentecostal leaders should encourage believers to ask questions, wrestle with doctrine, and engage in thoughtful reflection. Small groups, Bible studies, and discipleship programs

---

[60] Sire, *Habits of the Mind.*

[61] Sire, *Habits of the Mind.*

[62] Sire, *Habits of the Mind.*

can serve as platforms for this kind of intellectual engagement.

Second, Sire emphasizes the role of leadership in modeling intellectual humility and integrity.[63] Pentecostal pastors and teachers should not present themselves as possessing all the answers but should demonstrate a willingness to learn and grow. Open discussion of difficult theological questions and honest acknowledgment of uncertainty foster a culture of intellectual humility.

Third, Sire suggests that Pentecostal worship services should reflect a balance between emotional expression and theological instruction.[64] Spontaneous prayer and tongues should be balanced with structured teaching and biblical exposition. This creates a worship environment that engages both the heart and the mind.

Finally, Sire encourages Pentecostals to engage with the broader Christian intellectual tradition.[65] Reading church history, studying classical Christian texts, and engaging with contemporary theological scholarship can deepen Pentecostal theological understanding and strengthen the church's witness.

Sire's framework challenges Pentecostals to see the life of the mind as an essential dimension of worship. To think well is to worship well. The pursuit of truth, when guided by humility, perseverance, and integrity, becomes a sacred act. Pentecostals who cultivate these virtues will experience a deeper and more mature faith—one that engages both the heart and the mind in the worship of God.

Reflection Questions

1. How does Sire's framework of intellectual virtues challenge your understanding of Pentecostal worship?
2. In what ways can your church promote intellectual humility, perseverance, and integrity within its worship practices?

---

[63] Sire, *Habits of the Mind.*

[64] Sire, *Habits of the Mind.*

[65] Sire, *Habits of the Mind.*

3. How can intellectual engagement enhance your personal experience of worship?
4. What steps can Pentecostal leaders take to create a culture where theological questions and intellectual inquiry are encouraged?
5. How might cultivating intellectual virtues strengthen the broader Pentecostal witness in contemporary culture?

9

Yong and Coulter: Spirit Led Academic Formation

At the turn of the twenty-first century, a new generation of Pentecostal scholars began to reimagine the role of the Holy Spirit—not only as the agent of revival but as the animating presence within theological inquiry and academic formation. Among the most prominent of these voices are Amos Yong and Dale M. Coulter, who together represent a vital movement within Pentecostalism—one that seeks to recover the life of the mind without abandoning the Spirit-filled heart. Their work signals a theological and institutional shift: a call to reject the false dichotomy between charismatic experience and intellectual depth, and to rediscover how the Spirit empowers both.[66]

Emerging from traditions shaped by spontaneous revival, emotional fervor, and populist skepticism toward formal education, Pentecostalism has often privileged the immediacy of experience over the structure of theological reflection. But Yong and Coulter propose that this historic pattern is not a necessity—it is a distortion. In their view, the same Spirit who inspires tongues and healing also grants wisdom, nurtures understanding, and calls believers to think well. The Spirit is not only active in the altar call, but also

---

[66] Yong and Coulter, *Holy Spirit and Higher Education*.

in the classroom. The mind, they argue, is not a neutral vessel or a worldly distraction—it is a temple, capable of being indwelt, sanctified, and renewed by the Spirit of God.[67]

Drawing upon the rich resources of Christian theology, philosophy, and educational theory, Yong and Coulter present a vision of Spirit-empowered intellectual life as a form of discipleship. Their theological imagination is expansive: the Spirit is at work not only in personal piety and corporate worship but also in the pursuit of truth across every discipline. Whether one is engaging Scripture, probing the mysteries of the Trinity, or exploring questions in science or the arts, the Spirit remains the teacher. The life of the mind, rightly ordered, becomes not a rival to Pentecostal spirituality but its rightful companion—a means through which the believer comes to know and love God more fully.

In a moment when Pentecostalism continues to rise globally while struggling with theological depth and credibility, Yong and Coulter offer a model that is both prophetic and pastoral. They invite the Church to imagine worship that is as thoughtful as it is passionate, education that is as Spirit-led as it is rigorous, and discipleship that embraces the full range of human faculties. In doing so, they lay the groundwork for a Pentecostal future where reason and revelation no longer compete but converge under the guidance of the Spirit.

The Role of Pentecostal Higher Education

A key focus of Yong and Coulter's work is the role of Pentecostal higher education in fostering the integration of faith and intellect. They argue that Christian universities and seminaries have a unique opportunity to shape students in a way that combines academic rigor with deep spiritual formation. For Yong and Coulter, education is not merely about transmitting knowledge—it is about forming students in a "Spirit-infused habitus" where intellectual growth, moral development, and spiritual maturity are

---

[67] Yong and Coulter, *Holy Spirit and Higher Education*.

integrated.[68]

The concept of habitus reflects the formation of habitual patterns of thought, behavior, and devotion that shape a person's character and world-view. Yong and Coulter propose that Pentecostal educational institutions should intentionally cultivate a Spirit-infused habitus—an approach to learning where theological reflection, academic inquiry, and spiritual experience are woven together into a single formative process. This requires more than simply adding theological courses to a secular curriculum; it demands that the entire educational process be shaped by the conviction that the Spirit empowers the life of the mind.[69]

Pentecostal universities and seminaries, in this model, serve as laboratories for the integration of faith and reason. Yong and Coulter advocate for a curriculum that combines rigorous engagement with academic disciplines—philosophy, science, literature, and social sciences—with deep theological reflection and spiritual formation.[70] This integrated model of education enables students to explore complex moral and intellectual issues while remaining grounded in a Pentecostal understanding of the Spirit's work.

This approach also challenges the assumption that Pentecostal identity is primarily defined by charismatic experience. Yong and Coulter propose that theological depth and intellectual engagement are just as central to Pentecostal identity as speaking in tongues or prophetic utterance.[71] The Spirit who empowers miraculous gifts is the same Spirit who empowers wisdom, understanding, and theological discernment.

Yong and Coulter envision Pentecostal higher education not only as a means of equipping students for professional success but also as a formative process that shapes students into thoughtful, faithful, and Spirit-filled leaders. They argue that Pentecostal universities should serve as models of holistic formation, where students learn to engage with the complexities of modern

---

[68] Yong and Coulter, *Holy Spirit and Higher Education.*

[69] Yong and Coulter, *Holy Spirit and Higher Education.*

[70] Yong and Coulter, *Holy Spirit and Higher Education.*

[71] Yong and Coulter, *Holy Spirit and Higher Education.*

society from a position of both theological conviction and intellectual integrity.[72]

Overcoming Pentecostal Anti-Intellectualism

Yong and Coulter acknowledge that this vision faces significant challenges within the Pentecostal tradition. Historically, Pentecostalism has been shaped by revivalist and populist impulses that often viewed formal education and intellectual inquiry with suspicion. Early Pentecostals, influenced by leaders such as Charles Parham and William Seymour, prioritized spiritual immediacy over theological reflection. The spontaneous movement of the Spirit in worship was valued more highly than structured teaching or doctrinal consistency.

This anti-intellectual strain has left a lasting imprint on Pentecostal identity. In many Pentecostal communities, theological questions are met with skepticism, and intellectual exploration is viewed as a threat to faith. Yong and Coulter argue that overcoming this legacy requires a deliberate effort to cultivate a culture where faith and reason are seen as complementary rather than opposing forces.

They propose several strategies for addressing Pentecostal anti-intellectualism:[73]

1. **Developing Theologically Integrated Curricula** – Pentecostal institutions should create educational programs that integrate theological reflection with academic disciplines. Theology should not be isolated as a separate subject—it should shape the entire educational process, providing a framework for interpreting all forms of knowledge.
2. **Creating Spaces for Theological Inquiry** – Pentecostal communities should cultivate environments where theological questioning is encouraged rather than discouraged. Pastors, teachers, and leaders should

---

[72] Yong and Coulter, *Holy Spirit and Higher Education*.

[73] Yong and Coulter, *Holy Spirit and Higher Education*.

model intellectual humility and openness to learning. Questions and doubts should be treated as opportunities for deeper understanding rather than threats to faith.

3. **Engaging with Broader Christian Traditions** – Pentecostals should engage with the intellectual resources of the wider Christian tradition. Church history, classical theology, and contemporary scholarship provide valuable tools for theological reflection. Yong and Coulter argue that Pentecostals should view themselves as part of the broader Christian intellectual tradition rather than as an isolated movement.

4. **Balancing Spiritual Experience with Intellectual Depth** – Pentecostal worship should reflect both the immediacy of the Spirit's presence and the theological depth of Scripture and Christian tradition. Spontaneous expressions of praise and structured teaching should be woven together into a unified worship experience.

By addressing these challenges, Yong and Coulter believe that Pentecostal communities can reclaim the intellectual life as a vital dimension of worship and discipleship. The Spirit's work in the life of the mind is not a departure from Pentecostal identity—it is a fulfillment of it.[74]

Worship as a Space for Theological Reflection

Yong and Coulter's vision extends beyond higher education into the realm of congregational worship. They argue that Pentecostal worship should create space for both charismatic encounter and theological reflection. Emotional expressions of worship—such as speaking in tongues, prophecy, and spontaneous praise—should be balanced with structured teaching, reflective prayer, and theological instruction.[75]

This approach reflects the biblical model of worship. In 1 Corinthians 14, Paul instructs the Corinthian church to value both spiritual gifts and

---

[74] Yong and Coulter, *Holy Spirit and Higher Education.*

[75] Yong and Coulter, *Holy Spirit and Higher Education.*

intelligibility. Speaking in tongues and prophecy should be accompanied by interpretation and teaching so that the whole congregation may be edified. Yong and Coulter argue that this balance between spiritual immediacy and theological depth should characterize Pentecostal worship today.

For Yong and Coulter, this balance reflects the broader work of the Spirit in forming the church.[76] The Spirit's work includes both charismatic gifts and intellectual discernment. A church that prays with the spirit and with the understanding (1 Corinthians 14:15) reflects the fullness of the Spirit's activity. Pentecostal worship, when shaped by this balance, becomes a space where believers encounter the Spirit not only in emotional experience but also in theological reflection and intellectual discovery.

A Model for the Broader Church

Ultimately, Yong and Coulter present their vision as a model not only for Pentecostals but for the broader Christian community.[77] The integration of faith and reason, empowered by the Spirit, reflects the biblical vision of holistic worship and discipleship. Pentecostal institutions that embody this model can serve as examples for other Christian communities seeking to integrate theological depth with spiritual vitality.

This vision challenges Pentecostals to embrace the life of the mind as an essential dimension of faith. The Spirit's transformative work includes both emotional renewal and intellectual growth. A mature Pentecostal faith will engage both heart and mind, combining theological depth with charismatic experience. Yong and Coulter call Pentecostals to reclaim this integrated vision of worship and discipleship—a vision where the Spirit empowers both the emotional and intellectual dimensions of faith.[78]

---

[76] Yong and Coulter, *Holy Spirit and Higher Education*.

[77] Yong and Coulter, *Holy Spirit and Higher Education*.

[78] Yong and Coulter, *Holy Spirit and Higher Education*.

Reflection Questions

1. How does Yong and Coulter's vision challenge the historical anti-intellectualism within Pentecostalism?

2. In what ways can Pentecostal universities and seminaries integrate theological reflection with academic disciplines?

3. How can local Pentecostal churches balance charismatic experience with theological teaching in worship?

4. How does the concept of a "Spirit-infused habitus" apply to your own intellectual and spiritual formation?

5. How might embracing intellectual engagement strengthen Pentecostal witness to the broader culture?

10

Toward a Pentecostal Theology of Integrated Worship

From its earliest days, Pentecostalism has pulsed with spiritual vitality—born in storefront churches, prayer circles, and urban revivals where the unmediated power of the Holy Spirit transformed ordinary believers into bold witnesses. The movement's signature marks—speaking in tongues, prophetic utterance, healing, and ecstatic worship—signaled a faith rooted not in abstraction but in direct encounter. This embodied, experiential spirituality formed the core of Pentecostal identity. But it also came at a cost: a persistent suspicion of theological systems, formal education, and the life of the mind.

This tension has deep historical roots. Emerging from the Holiness revivals of the late 19th century, early Pentecostalism inherited an anti-institutional ethos that regarded seminaries as spiritually lifeless and theological discourse as potentially stifling to the Spirit. Leaders like Charles Fox Parham and William J. Seymour prioritized immediacy over order, favoring spontaneous revelation over sustained study. Their eschatological urgency—fueled by a strong belief in Christ's imminent return—discouraged long-term theological formation in favor of Spirit-led immediacy and moral readiness. In such a framework, thinking too long or studying too deeply was seen as a distraction from the work of the Spirit and the pressing call to prepare for the coming

King.

Theologically, Pentecostalism's emphasis on being "led by the Spirit" further contributed to the suspicion of intellectual engagement. The fear that study might "quench the Spirit" created a sharp divide between charismatic experience and theological reflection. Structured or intellectually guided worship was often perceived as less authentic, less alive to the movement of the Spirit.

Practically, this tension was reinforced by limitations in leadership formation. Pentecostal pastors were often trained in Bible schools or seminaries that emphasized either doctrinal depth or spiritual power, but seldom both. As a result, many leaders were well-equipped to facilitate dynamic, emotionally resonant worship but lacked the tools to guide their congregations into sustained theological reflection. Worship resources mirrored these extremes—either leaning toward rigid liturgy or untethered emotional expression—leaving little room for a truly integrated approach.

The result has been a deep and enduring divide. On one side: emotional fervor, spiritual gifts, and passionate worship. On the other: theological inquiry, critical thinking, and doctrinal clarity. Too often, Pentecostal worship has forced a choice between these dimensions. The fire of revival has seemed incompatible with the discipline of theological study; the immediacy of the Spirit at odds with the rigors of the mind. Thankfully, progress has been made in this arena within the more charismatic wings of the convergence movement.[79]

And so we see, this divide is neither biblical nor inevitable. It is the legacy of a particular historical moment, not a permanent feature of Pentecostal spirituality. Today, as Pentecostalism expands across the globe and gains influence in academic and ecumenical contexts, a new horizon is emerging— one where Spirit and understanding are no longer in opposition. What if Pentecostal worship could be both intellectually rich and spiritually alive?

---

[79] See for example the worship services at The House That Love Built, Vineland, NJ; Christ International Church, Orlando, FL; and The Cathedral at the Gathering Place, Rochester, NY

What if theological reflection and charismatic experience could converge in a vision of truly integrated worship?

It is toward this possibility that we now turn.

The Opportunity of Integration

Despite the challenges mentioned above, the integration of intellectual engagement and charismatic worship presents a profound opportunity for Pentecostalism. Far from being in conflict, intellectual depth and charismatic expression can function as complementary dimensions of authentic Christian worship. An integrated Pentecostal worship model values both the immediacy of the Spirit's presence and the theological depth that comes from studying and reflecting on God's truth.

Integration allows Pentecostals to engage the broader Christian tradition while preserving their distinctive charismatic identity. Pentecostalism's emphasis on the Spirit's work resonates with the historic Christian understanding of the Spirit as the source of wisdom and understanding. The same Spirit who inspires tongues and prophecy also inspires theological insight and intellectual discovery. By reclaiming this connection, Pentecostals can position themselves as a bridge between the charismatic and intellectual dimensions of the Christian faith.

Furthermore, an integrated worship model equips Pentecostals to engage more effectively with the complex moral, social, and theological challenges of the contemporary world. The emotional intensity of Pentecostal worship provides a powerful foundation for spiritual resilience, while theological depth offers the critical tools needed to navigate cultural and philosophical challenges. A Pentecostalism that combines charismatic fervor with intellectual rigor will be better equipped to provide a coherent and credible witness in a pluralistic and secular society.

This synthesis also strengthens the internal life of the church. A worship culture that values both emotional experience and theological reflection creates a more stable and mature faith community. Worshipers who engage both their hearts and minds in worship will be less prone to emotional burnout and theological confusion. A balanced worship model fosters spiritual depth and resilience, producing believers who are emotionally authentic and theologically grounded.

A Biblical Framework for Integrated Worship

The foundation for a Pentecostal theology of integrated worship is found in Scripture, particularly in the Great Commandment and Paul's exhortation to the Corinthians.

The Great Commandment – A Holistic Vision of Worship

In Mark 12:30, Jesus calls believers to "love the Lord your God with all your heart, and with all your soul, and with all your mind, and with all your strength." This commandment presents a holistic vision of worship that engages the entire person—emotional, spiritual, intellectual, and physical. Pentecostal worship has historically excelled at engaging the heart and the strength—expressing love for God through emotional and physical acts of worship. However, the inclusion of the mind in the Great Commandment challenges Pentecostals to incorporate theological reflection and intellectual engagement into their worship practices.

1 Corinthians 14:15 – Praying with the Spirit and Understanding

Paul's instruction to the Corinthian church further underscores the importance of balancing charismatic experience with intellectual reflection. "I will pray with the spirit, but I will also pray with the understanding; I will sing with the spirit, but I will also sing with the understanding." Paul affirms the value of both charismatic expression and theological discernment. For Pentecostals, this passage provides a biblical mandate to integrate emotional and intellectual dimensions in worship. To pray and sing with understanding means that theological depth and intellectual reflection are not obstacles to worship but essential dimensions of it.

The Role of the Holy Spirit in Integration

Central to this theological framework is the pneumatological conviction that the Holy Spirit serves as the unifying force in worship. The Spirit's role is not to elevate emotional expression over theological reflection or vice versa, but to guide believers into a worship experience where intellect and charisma function in harmony.

The Spirit empowers both the emotional and intellectual dimensions of worship. The same Spirit who inspires tongues and healing also inspires theological insight and moral discernment. The Spirit's work in worship is not limited to emotional expressions of praise—it includes the illumination of Scripture, the cultivation of wisdom, and the deepening of theological understanding.

The Spirit enables believers to approach theological reflection with humility and worship with intentionality. An integrated Pentecostal worship experience reflects the Spirit's capacity to form believers into whole persons—capable of loving God with heart, soul, mind, and strength.

Some Strategies for Implementing Integrated Worship

Balanced Worship Structures

Pentecostal churches can begin cultivating integrated worship by designing services that intentionally blend reflective and experiential elements. This means creating space not only for the spontaneous movements of the Spirit—such as prophetic declarations, extended moments of singing in tongues, or spontaneous intercession—but also for structured acts of worship that guide the mind and shape theological understanding. Practices like corporate prayer, creedal recitation, and Scripture-based liturgical readings do not quench the Spirit; rather, they offer a theological anchor that grounds the emotional vitality of Pentecostal worship in the larger story of the Church and the revealed truth of Scripture.

Incorporating both form and freedom in worship helps create an environment that values emotional authenticity and intellectual engagement. The structure offers a rhythm that sustains the congregation's attention and deepens their awareness of God's presence, while charismatic expressions allow space for Spirit-led responsiveness and personal encounter. The result is a worship culture that welcomes both silence and shouting, both deep reflection and exuberant praise, affirming that the Spirit moves in many ways—and often moves most powerfully where heart and mind are aligned in devotion.

Theological Education for Pentecostal Leaders

The integration of intellect and Spirit in worship must begin with leadership formation. Pentecostal pastors and worship leaders must be trained not only to steward the gifts of the Spirit but also to think theologically and reflect critically. This requires a reimagining of seminary and Bible school curricula. Rather than isolating theology in the classroom and worship in the chapel, Pentecostal institutions should model integration—offering spaces where students engage in vibrant, Spirit-filled worship while also wrestling deeply with Scripture, church history, and theological tradition.

Kerygma University[80] exemplifies this kind of holistic formation through its use of the Competency-Based Theological Education (CBTE) model, which integrates Spirit-empowered worship, theological reflection, and contextual ministry training. By aligning academic rigor with vocational relevance and spiritual depth, Kerygma cultivates leaders who are equipped to serve the church with both power and wisdom.

This kind of formation produces leaders who are both spiritually sensitive and intellectually equipped—able to preach prophetically and teach with clarity, to pray in tongues and also articulate sound doctrine. When Pentecostal leaders embody this balance, they model a more mature expression of the

---

[80] KerygmaUniversity.org - The Author is the President of the University.

faith, inviting their congregations into a deeper, more holistic engagement with God. The church cannot move toward integrated worship without leaders who themselves have been shaped by both the fire of the Spirit and the wisdom of the Word. Institutions like Kerygma University are charting a path forward, demonstrating how Pentecostal education can be both academically excellent and spiritually alive.

Theological Framing of Charismatic Practices

One of the most practical ways to cultivate integrated worship is through theological framing—helping congregants understand the biblical and doctrinal significance of charismatic practices. Too often, Pentecostal believers experience gifts like tongues, prophecy, or healing without a deeper grasp of their meaning, origin, or purpose. When these practices are framed theologically, they are no longer just emotional phenomena but expressions of God's self-revelation and the Church's vocation in the world.

Pastors and worship leaders play a vital role in this process. By teaching regularly on the gifts of the Spirit, grounding them in Scripture, and connecting them to the broader narrative of redemption, leaders help congregants see these gifts not as spiritual novelties but as means of grace—tools for edification, evangelism, and ecclesial maturity. Explaining why we speak in tongues, why prophecy is vital, and how healing functions within the kingdom mission elevates worship beyond feeling to faithful understanding. This doesn't diminish the power of the gifts—it clarifies and amplifies their purpose.

Developing Integrated Worship Resources

Finally, Pentecostal communities must be intentional about creating and curating worship resources that reflect this integrated vision. Too often, the songs we sing, the prayers we pray, and the devotionals we read reflect either theological abstraction or charismatic spontaneity—but rarely both. What's needed is a new generation of worship material that blends theological richness with spiritual intensity, head and heart, Scripture and Spirit.

Songwriters, liturgists, and pastors can collaborate to produce resources that reflect Pentecostal convictions while drawing from the broader Christian tradition. A worship guide might pair a time of free praise with a reading from the creeds. A new song might be grounded in Trinitarian theology while leaving space for Spirit-led intercession. Devotionals and discipleship materials can encourage daily engagement with both Scripture and the gifts of the Spirit. These kinds of resources will not only shape weekly services but will form a generation of believers who know how to worship with both understanding and unction.

The Future of Pentecostal Worship

The integration of intellectual engagement and charismatic worship is not merely an academic ideal—it is a pastoral imperative. It is a call to maturity, a summons to wholeness, and a vital task for the Pentecostal movement's continued growth, credibility, and fruitfulness. The future of Pentecostal worship depends not only on our ability to sustain revival fire but on our willingness to steward that fire with theological clarity and spiritual wisdom. To worship God in spirit and in truth, as Jesus taught, is to refuse the false choice between emotional passion and doctrinal depth. It is to embrace a worship that engages the whole person—heart, soul, mind, and strength.

At the center of this renewal lies a rediscovery of the Great Commandment. Pentecostals have long excelled in loving God with heart and strength—demonstrating passion, energy, and deep spiritual hunger. But loving God with the mind is just as central to Christian devotion. To study is to love. To reflect is to revere. To teach well is to worship deeply. Our churches must become places where theological reflection and charismatic expression are not only welcomed but expected—where the move of the Spirit includes both tongues and teaching, both fervent praise and thoughtful proclamation.

The future of Pentecostal worship will require leaders who can model this integration. It is not enough to preach with fire if we cannot teach with faithfulness. It is not enough to stir the emotions if we cannot anchor the soul. Pentecostal pastors and worship leaders must be equipped to nurture communities where the Holy Spirit moves freely and Scripture is handled rightly. This means investing in the formation of leaders who have been shaped both by the Spirit's power and by sound theological training. Institutions like **Kerygma University**, through their **Competency-Based Theological Education (CBTE)** model, are showing us what this looks like—training leaders who are contextually aware, biblically grounded, spiritually attuned, and missionally engaged.

Such integration does not diminish the Pentecostal witness; it strengthens it. A worship culture that is both emotionally vibrant and theologically mature will cultivate disciples who are rooted, resilient, and ready to engage the complexities of the world. It will produce believers who are not swayed by every wind of doctrine, nor worn out by emotional extremes, but who walk in both Spirit and wisdom. Integrated worship creates space for the Spirit to work in the intellect, just as powerfully as He does in the emotions or the body. When we pray and sing with the understanding as well as the spirit, we become whole worshipers—and whole worshipers are what the world most desperately needs.

Externally, this renewal will enhance the credibility and witness of Pentecostal churches in a skeptical and often hostile culture. A faith that can speak in tongues and speak into culture—articulately, wisely, and faithfully—will resonate beyond the walls of the sanctuary. Integrated worship enables Pentecostals to take their place in the broader Christian tradition, not as outliers or anomalies, but as Spirit-led theologians, pastors, artists, and scholars who contribute to the flourishing of the whole Church. It is time for Pentecostals to bring both our fire and our insight to the table—to offer not only revival but renewal, not only testimony but theological vision.

But this is not something that will happen by default. It must be pursued with prayerful intention, courageous leadership, and a renewed vision of what it means to be Pentecostal. Churches must begin rethinking their worship services, retooling their discipleship pathways, and reshaping their educational priorities. Seminaries must resist the pull of compartmentalized training and embrace models that form the whole person. Pastors must study.

Scholars must worship. Worship leaders must teach. And the people of God must be invited to love the Lord not only with feeling but with fullness.

This is not a retreat from Pentecostal distinctiveness—it is a recovery of it. The Pentecostal tradition has always been about fullness—full gospel, full surrender, full empowerment. Integrated worship simply presses that vision further, calling for a fullness that includes the mind alongside the heart. It is a call to become fully human in our devotion, to offer God nothing less than the entirety of ourselves, formed by Scripture, filled with the Spirit, and framed by the wisdom of the Church.

This is the future toward which we must labor, preach, teach, and pray—a Pentecostalism that is as thoughtful as it is passionate, as rooted as it is radiant. When we hold together the head and the heart, the classroom and the altar, the creed and the cry, we become what the Spirit has always intended us to be: worshipers in spirit and in truth.

Reflection Questions

1. How does the Great Commandment shape your understanding of holistic worship?
2. What are the barriers to intellectual engagement in your church's worship practices?
3. How can Pentecostal leaders cultivate a balance between emotional expression and theological depth?
4. How might integrated worship enhance Pentecostal engagement with the broader Christian tradition?
5. How can the Holy Spirit's role in both emotional and intellectual formation be emphasized in Pentecostal worship?

Bibliography

Charry, Ellen T. "Educating for Wisdom: Theological Studies as a Spiritual Exercise." *Theology Today* 66, no. 3 (October 2009): 295–308. https://doi.org /10.1177/004057360906600303.

Di Ceglie, Roberto. "A Sacrificial View of Life." *Religions* 14, no. 7 (July 5, 2023): 876. https://doi.org/10.3390/rel14070876.

Elders, Leo. "The Aristotelian Commentaries of St. Thomas Aquinas." *The Review of Metaphysics* 63, no. 1 (2009): 29–53. https://www.jstor.org/stable/ 40387727.

GotQuestions.org. "Who Was Charles Parham?," August 14, 2024. https://w ww.gotquestions.org/Charles-Parham.html.

Jeon Ahn Yongnan. *Interpretation of Tongues and Prophecy in 1 Corinthians 12-14, with a Pentecostal Hermeneutics.* BRILL, 2019. https://brill-com.dtl.id m.oclc.org/display/title/54127.

Kerygma University. "Home," 2023. https://kerygmauniversity.org/.

Lee, Jeong-In, and Jangwan Ko. "From Rational Inquiry to Sacred Insight: The Role of Religion in Augustine's Views on Liberal Education." *Religions* 15, no. 1 (January 17, 2024): 122. https://doi.org/10.3390/rel15010122.

Mouw, Richard J. *Called to the Life of the Mind.* Wm. B. Eerdmans Publishing, 2014.

Nanez, Rick M. *Full Gospel, Fractured Minds? : A Call to Use God's Gift of the Intellect.* Grand Rapids, Mich.: Zondervan ; Enfield, 2006.

Nel, Marius. "Development of Theological Training and Hermeneutics in Pentecostalism: A Historical Perspective and Analysis." *Studia Historiae Ecclesiasticae (SHE)* 42, no. 2 (2016). https://doi.org/10.17159/2412-4265/2 016/1322.

O'Reilly, Kevin E. "The Significance of Worship in the Thought of Thomas

Aquinas." *International Philosophical Quarterly* 53, no. 4 (2013): 453–62. https://doi.org/10.5840/ipq201353444.

Revelation Lad. "Why Does Jesus' Wording of the Shema Include the Addition of 'and with All Your Mind?'" Biblical Hermeneutics Stack Exchange, May 29, 2018. https://hermeneutics.stackexchange.com/questions/33262/why-does-jesus-wording-of-the-shema-include-the-addition-of-and-with-all-your/54162#54162.

Sire, James W. *Habits of the Mind*. InterVarsity Press, 2022.

Stein, Robert H. *Mark (Baker Exegetical Commentary on the New Testament)*. Grand Rapids: Baker Academic, 2008. https://ebookcentral-proquest-com.dtl.idm.oclc.org/lib/dtl/detail.action?docID=4446284..

Tan, Kim Huat. "The Shema and Early Christianity." *Tyndale Bulletin* 59, no. 2 (November 1, 2008). https://doi.org/10.53751/001c.29256.

Yong, Amos, and Dale M Coulter. *The Holy Spirit and Higher Education*. Waco, TX: Baylor University Press, 2023.

Forming the Whole Person for the Whole Church

The integration of Spirit and understanding, passion and depth, is more than an idea—it is a movement. And at the forefront of that movement stands Kerygma University, an institution rooted in the conviction that theological education must form the whole person: mind, heart, soul, and strength. In a time when the Church urgently needs leaders who can think clearly, live faithfully, and minister powerfully, Kerygma University is answering the call by reimagining what Spirit-empowered education can look like.

Founded with a vision to serve the global Church—especially underserved Afro-Latino communities—Kerygma University offers affordable, accessible, and accredited theological education that is both academically rigorous and spiritually vibrant. Through its partnership with the Kairos University global network, Kerygma offers pathways to government-recognized degrees while maintaining a contextualized, Spirit-sensitive approach to formation. The result is a learning environment where intellectual discovery and charismatic devotion do not compete—they complement.

At the heart of Kerygma's educational model is Competency-Based Theological Education (CBTE). Unlike traditional models that measure progress by time in a classroom, CBTE measures formation through demonstrated growth. Students at Kerygma are guided by mentor teams—Faculty Mentors, Vocational Mentors, and Personal Mentors—who walk with them throughout their journey. These mentors invest deeply in students' spiritual life, theological reflection, and practical ministry skills, ensuring that formation happens in community and leads to transformation.

But Kerygma University is not just preparing pastors and theologians—it is raising up Spirit-filled reformers. Its graduates are thinkers and worshipers, church planters and scholars, prophets and bridge-builders. Whether serving in local congregations, launching new ministries, or engaging the culture through counseling, education, or advocacy, Kerygma students are equipped to love God with all their minds and all their hearts.

Courses at Kerygma are designed to reflect this integration. Students wrestle with the Great Tradition, engage Scripture deeply, and reflect on contemporary challenges through the lens of Spirit-filled theology. Worship and study are never separated; learning is framed as an act of discipleship and devotion. In every course, the goal is not simply knowledge acquisition, but whole-person formation for the sake of God's mission.

Kerygma's distinctive approach makes theological education not only possible but personal. With monthly tuition capped at $300 for most degrees, students receive everything they need—courses, mentoring, books, and access to a global community—without crippling debt. And because learning happens within the student's ministry context, the classroom is never removed from real-life service. Students grow where they are planted, and their ministries flourish as they grow.

The word *kerygma* means proclamation—specifically, the proclamation of the gospel. At Kerygma University, this proclamation shapes everything: not just what we teach, but how we teach, whom we teach, and why we teach. To proclaim Christ and to instruct his Church—this is the mission. And this mission aligns perfectly with the vision laid out in this book: a Pentecostal theology of integrated worship that holds together passion and intellect, doctrine and devotion, Spirit and truth.

Kerygma University exists for those who believe that worship should be both deep and wide, both joyful and wise. It exists for leaders who are hungry not just for inspiration but for formation. It exists for the church—especially the parts of the church that have been overlooked or under-resourced. And it exists for such a time as this.

To learn more, apply, or partner with us, visit www.kerygmauniversity.org. The Spirit is calling. The Church is waiting. And the mind, when formed by the Spirit and the Word, is ready to worship.

www.ingramcontent.com/pod-product-compliance
Lightning Source LLC
Chambersburg PA
CBHW071748090426
42738CB00011B/2601